BLUE WHALES

THE WHALE DISCOVERY LIBRARY

Sarah Palmer

Illustrated by David Palmer

Rourke Enterprises, Inc.
Vero Beach, Florida 32964

Library of Congress Cataloging-in-Publication Data

Palmer, Sarah, 1955-
 Blue Whales.

 (The Whale discovery library)
 Includes index.
 Summary: Intoduces the physical appearance,
habits, diet and habitat of the blue whale and
threats to its existence.
 1. Blue Whale—Juvenile literature. [1. Blue
Whale. 2. Whales] I. Title. II. Series:
Palmer, Sarah, 1955-
Whale discovery library.
QL737.C424P34 1989   599.5'1   88-3239
ISBN 0-86592-480-5

TABLE OF CONTENTS

BLUE WHALES

Blue whales are baleen whales which do not have any teeth. They take water containing tiny shrimp-like creatures in through the front of their mouth. Then the whales push the water back out into the ocean through the side of their mouth. The **baleen plates** in the side of the blue whale's mouth act like a strainer. They let the water out and keep the food in the whale's mouth.

Blue whales are the largest animals in the world

HOW THEY LOOK

Blue whales are the largest animals ever known. They are even bigger than most of the biggest dinosaurs. Blue whales can grow as long as 100 feet. Some weigh almost 160 tons. A full-grown blue whale has over 300 baleen plates on each side of his mouth. Blue whales have a dark, slate-blue back, with light colored flecks.
The underside is pale.

*A blue whale blows at t
surface of the ocean*

WHERE THEY LIVE

Blue whales can be found in three different places. Some live in the Antarctic Ocean. Others live in the North Atlantic and North Pacific Oceans. In the winter, blue whales **migrate** to warmer waters. They eat very little during their stay in warm waters. Blue whales are always the first whales to return to the cold **polar** waters in the spring. There they always find a lot to eat.

*Blue whales spend half the year
in cold, polar oceans*

WHAT THEY EAT

Like all baleen whales, blue whales live mainly on small shrimp-like creatures called **krill**. The krill is taken in with water from the ocean. It is swallowed after the whale has strained the water out from his mouth through the baleen plates. Blue whales eat a ton of krill in one mouthful. They are so big that they have to eat many tons of food each day.

Blue whales eat small creatures called krill

Today it is unusual to see more
than three blue whales together

Blue whales are baleen whales

LIVING IN THE OCEAN

Much of the blue whales' time is spent feeding. The whales that live in the Antarctic Ocean grow bigger than the ones found in the northern oceans. Scientists believe there may be more food for the whales in the Antarctic Ocean. The food may also be richer in **vitamins**. The blue whales that live in the north have separate lives from those in the south. They never meet, even when both groups migrate to warmer waters.

Blue whales eat tons of krill and plankton each day

BABY BLUE WHALES

Blue whales are as big as some full-grown whales when they are born. An average blue whale **calf** is 23 feet long and weighs over 5 tons at birth. Calves drink only their mothers' milk for the first six months of their life. The milk is rich in vitamins and the calf grows very quickly. Blue whale calves grow a surprising 2 inches and 200 pounds each day during this time.

Baby blue whales grow very quickly

BLUE WHALES AND PEOPLE

Whales used to be hunted with a harpoon, a kind of spear attached to a rope. The **whalers** threw the harpoon at the whale and anchored it in its skin. But blue whales are so strong that they easily pulled away. Not many blue whales were caught in the early days of whaling. When the whalers began to use the **harpoon gun** in 1868, even the blue whales could no longer escape.

A whaler shoots a blue whale with a harpoon gun

SAVING BLUE WHALES

Blue whales were prized for their **blubber**. This thick layer of fat under the skin was boiled down to make **blubber oil**, also called **whale oil**. Blue whales have more blubber than most whales. The blubber from an average blue whale makes between 10 and 20 tons of oil. The most oil ever made from a blue whale was 50 tons. So many blue whales were killed by whalers that very few are left. Now no one is allowed to kill blue whales.

Blue whales were the whalers' favorite whales

FACT FILE

Common Name: Blue Whale
Scientific Name: Balaenoptera musculus
Type: Baleen whale
Color: Dark slate-blue
Size: up to 100 feet
Weight: up to 155 tons
Number in World: 14,000

Glossary

baleen plates (BAL een PLATES) — whalebones used to strain food in a whale's mouth

blubber (BLUB ber) — a thick layer of fat beneath a whale's skin

blubber oil/whale oil (BLUB ber OIL/WHALE OIL) — the oil made from a whale's fat.

calf (CALF) — a baby whale

harpoon gun (har POON GUN) — a spear-gun used in hunting whales

krill (KRILL) — tiny shrimp-like creatures on which whales feed

to migrate (MI grate) — to move from one place to another, usually at the same time each year

polar (POL ar) — close to the North or South Pole

vitamins (VI ta mins) — substances needed for healthy growth

whalers (WHAL ers) — people who hunt whales

INDEX